Tell Me Abou[t]

ISLAMI[C] HISTORY

Pages from Islamic History

A beautiful silver *dirham* from the time of the Ilkhanid sultan Abu Sa'id (1316-1335 C.E.). The *kalimah* is inscribed in a square in Kufi script. The names of the four *al-khulafa' al-rashidun* are outside the square.

Written & Illustrated by
Luqman Nagy

Goodwordkidz

Two ceramic lustre tiles produced in Baghdad and sent as a gift to beautify the *mihrab* of the Sidi 'Uqba ibn Nafi Mosque in Qayrawan (Tunisia) in the 9th century CE.

First published 2003
Reprinted 2012

Goodword Books
1, Nizamuddin West Market
New Delhi-110 013
Tel. 9111-4182-7083, 4652-1511
Fax: 9111-4565-1771
email: info@goodwordbooks.com
www.goodwordbooks.com
www.goodword.net

Islamic Vision Ltd.
434 Coventry Road, Small Heath
Birmingham B10 0UG, U.K.
Tel. 121-773-0137
Fax: 121-766-8577
e-mail: info@ipci-iv.co.uk
www.islamicvision.co.uk

IB Publisher Inc.
81 Bloomingdale Rd, Hicksville
NY 11801, USA
Tel. 516-933-1000, Fax: 516-933-1200
Toll Free: 1-888-560-3222
email: info@ibpublisher.com
www.ibpublisher.com

Printed in India

This book is dedicated to its first three readers:
my children ‘Abd al-Haq, Meryem, & ‘Abd al-Hay.

Until the final surrender of the Nasrid capital of Granada to the Catholic monarchs in 1492 CE, Nasrid rulers of southern Al-Andalus continued to mint coins bearing the humble motto of their dynasty: *wa la ghaliba ila Allah* (“And there is no Victor but Allah”). Five hundred years later, this square silver half *dirham* still eloquently pro-claims their sincerity as Muslims.

CONTENTS

بسم الله الرحمن الرحيم

INTRODUCTION

It is often said that "A nation remains alive when its culture and history remain alive." Every nation, therefore, seeks to know and preserve its history and cultural legacy. Islamic history, the story of events involving the lives of countless Muslims (and, of course, their interactions with non-Muslims too) over a period of more than 1,400 years is a vast book with chapters describing sublime achievements as well as tragic failures.

From the very birth of Islam, Muslims have been admonished to be literate and knowledgeable. To fully understand ourselves as members of one great *ummah* - with all our multi-ethnic origins, linguistic diversity and immense geographic spread – we must seek an honest understanding of our rich past. It is, therefore, the belief of the author that history *does* matter, to all of us.

The present work is a humble effort towards that aim. The lessons contained herein are intended mainly for young Muslims, especially those living in the West. Ten critical events in Islamic history have been presented chronologically. This book does not claim in any way to be a comprehensive survey of any particular time period of Islamic history. Events have been selected for their inherent overall importance and interest. The book ends arbitrarily with the fateful year 1492 CE. Undoubtedly, equally crucial historically important events could also have been identified in the past five hundred years.

Each chapter concludes with a set of comprehension questions and a topic for discussion. These of course can be supplemented by teacher and/or parent. Historically-accurate, full-colour illustrations attempt to contextualize the events discussed.

Finally, it is hoped that this book will encourage all its readers to continue their study of Islamic history in greater depth in order to comprehend not only our collective past,but also our future, *insha'Allah*.

To you all, my warmest salaams.

Luqman Nagy
King Fahd University
Dhahran, Saudi Arabia
April 2003

1. The Prophet's Letter - 628 CE

Allah sent the Prophet Muhammad ﷺ as a mercy to all mankind. The message of Islam was meant for all people: Arabs, Africans, Persians, Romans and Turks. During his lifetime, the Prophet ﷺ invited young and old, friend and foe, to the religion of peace, *din al-haq al-islam.*

After the Treaty of Hudaybiyah in 628 CE, more and more people in Arabia were embracing Islam and travelling to Madinah to pledge allegiance to the Prophet ﷺ. Muhammad ﷺ spoke to his Companions in Madinah:

> *O, people! Allah has sent me as the one who is compassionate to mankind and as the prophet to the world. Therefore, preach (the message of Islam) on my behalf; Allah will have mercy upon you...*

The Prophet ﷺ, therefore, decided to send Companions with letters to powerful rulers of his day such as the emperors of Byzantium and Persia, and the king of Ethiopia. Three of these letters of invitation to Islam have been preserved to this day.

The story of Heraclius is an interesting one. He was the ruler of the vast Byzantine Empire, the true superpower of his day. His capital was the beautiful city of Constantinople (present-day Istanbul, Turkey).

In 628 CE, Heraclius and his army had defeated in battle the second superpower of his day, the Persian Empire of Khusraw II.

Heraclius was in Homs (Syria) when he received the Prophet's ﷺ letter from his Companion Dihyah ibn Khalifah al-Kalbi (*radhi Allah-u 'anhu*). The contents of the letter read as follows:

> *In the name of Allah, the Beneficient, the Merciful. This letter is from Muhammad, the slave of Allah and His messenger to Heraclius, the ruler of the Byzantines. Peace be upon him who follows the right path. Furthermore, I invite you to Islam and if you become a Muslim, you will be safe, and Allah will double your reward, but if you reject this invitation to Islam, you will be committing a sin by misguiding your subjects. And I recite to you Allah's statement:*
>
> *"O, people of the scriptures (Jews and Christians)! Come to a word common to you and us that we worship none but Allah and that we associate no partners with Him and that none of us shall take others as lords besides Allah. Then if*

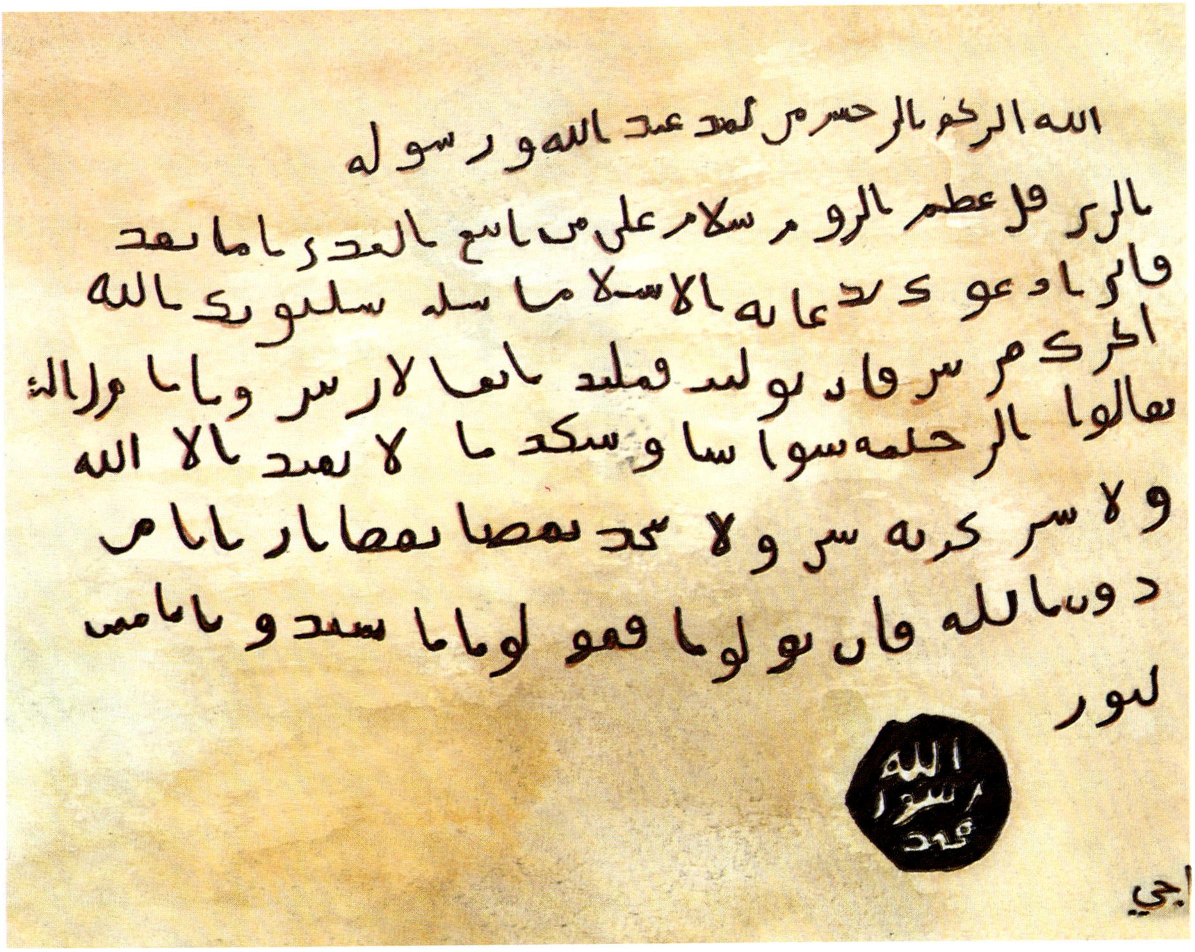
الله الرحمن الرحيم من محمد عبد الله ورسوله
الى هرقل عظيم الروم سلام على من اتبع الهدى اما بعد
فاني ادعوك بدعايه الاسلام اسلم تسلم يوتك الله
اجرك مرتين فان توليت فعليك اثم الاريسين ويا اهل الكتب
تعالوا الى كلمه سوا بيننا وبينكم الا نعبد الا الله
ولا نشرك به شيا ولا يتخذ بعضنا بعضا اربابا من
دون الله فان تولوا فقولوا اشهدوا بانا مسلمون
لبور
الله
رسول
محمد
اجي

they turn away, say: Bear witness that we are Muslims." (surah 3, ayah 64)

The letter was written on parchment and was stamped with the Prophet's ﷺ seal: *Muhammad Rasul Allah*. The letter to Heraclius is reproduced here.

After reading this letter, Heraclius sent soldiers to search the land for someone from the Prophet's ﷺ tribe. At the time, Abu Sufyan, the leader of the Quraysh, was on a trading mission in Gaza, Palestine. *Sahih Bukhari* discusses the meeting that took place between Abu Sufyan, still a bitter enemy of the Prophet ﷺ, and the emperor Heraclius.

Heraclius asked many questions about the Prophet's ﷺ character. Abu Sufyan could not deny that the Prophet ﷺ was an honest man who ordered his followers to pray, speak the truth and keep good relations with family members. Abu Sufyan added: "By Allah! Had I not been afraid of my companions labeling me a liar, I would not have spoken the truth about the Prophet ﷺ."

Heraclius truly believed that Muhammad ﷺ was the Prophet of Allah and said to his own people:

O, Byzantines! If success is your desire and if you seek right guidance and want your empire to remain, then give your pledge of allegiance to this Prophet (i.e. embrace Islam).

On hearing this, the Byzantines became very annoyed and angry. Heraclius now understood his own people's deep-seated hatred of Islam and that he, as their emperor, could not become a Muslim.

Heraclius left Syria for his capital, Constantinople. As he rode north, he glanced back and said: "Farewell for the last time, o land of Syria!" Heraclius knew that Islam would soon become the religion of all *balad al-sham* (present-day Syria, Palestine, Jordan and Lebanon).

In his lifetime, the Prophet's ﷺ invitation to *din al-haq al-islam* was accepted by just one ruler: the wise Nagus of Ethiopia, *al-Hamdulillah*. After a few years, however, the once mighty empires of Heraclius and Khusraw II along with Egypt all became Muslim lands, *masha'Allah*.

QUESTIONS

1. To whom was the message of Islam sent?

2. What did Muhammad ﷺ tell his Companions in Madinah after the Treaty of Hudaybiyah?

3. To whom were letters of invitation to Islam sent?

4. Who were the two superpowers during the time of the Prophet ﷺ?

5. Who was Heraclius and what was his capital city?

6. Where did Heraclius receive the Prophet's ﷺ letter?

7. What *ayah* did the Prophet ﷺ include in his letter?

8. What did Abu Sufyan tell Heraclius?

9. Why didn't Heraclius become a Muslim?

10. What leader *did* accept Islam after receiving a letter from the Prophet ﷺ?

Topic for Discussion: Why do you think it is important today to know about Muhammad's ﷺ letters of invitation to Islam? What valuable lessons can we learn from this *sunnah*?

2. 'Uqba ibn Nafi - Qayrawan 670 CE

One generation after the Prophet ﷺ, Muslims had brought the message of Islam to many distant lands, both to the east and west of Arabia.

In 670 CE, the Umayyad Caliph Mu'awiya with his capital in Damascus, sent 'Uqba ibn Nafi to govern the new province of *Ifriqiya* (present-day Tunisia). 'Uqba ibn Nafi arrived there with an army including many *sahaba (radhi Allah-u 'anhum)*, faithful Companions of the Prophet ﷺ. On an open plain, distant from the mountains and the sea, 'Uqba set up an army encampment. He wanted to build a city there that would be a "strong centre of Islam until the end of time." The city he established he called *Qayrawan* (Arabic for "camp").

Qayrawan grew into a very important city of Islamic learning and became the fourth holiest city after Makkah, Madinah and Jerusalem. An interesting legend surrounds the founding of Qayrawan. It is said that a horse from the army of 'Uqba ibn Nafi stumbled on a golden goblet buried in the earth. When it was uncovered, a spring appeared gushing water from the same source as the well of *zam zam* in Holy Makkah. From that day on, Qayrawan became a very special site of *ziyarah* for the Muslims of North Africa. It is still a city visited by Muslims the world over.

When Qayrawan became the capital of *Ifriqiya,* 'Uqba ibn Nafi built a mosque and a government house (*dar al-imara*) there. The Great Mosque, also called the Sidi 'Uqba Mosque, became a centre of Islamic science. The mosque had an important library of Arabic manuscripts. Many beautiful copies of the Holy Qur'an were hand-written in Qayrawan; some of these survive to this day in museums. The Sidi 'Uqba Mosque is one of the most beautiful examples of Islamic architecture. Its exterior and interior are important for several reasons.

The Great Mosque of Qayrawan was built using marble columns and stone taken from old Roman and Byzantine ruins. The three-story minaret (see illustration) is the oldest surviving minaret in the world! From the top of this minaret, one can view the entire walled city of old Qayrawan and the fertile plain lying outside it.

Inside the Mosque of Sidi 'Uqba, there are many priceless treasures of Islamic art. The exquisite wooden *minbar* (pulpit) was made by master craftsmen in Iraq and sent to Qayrawan as a gift to the city in 862 CE. It is, therefore, one of the oldest examples of a carved wooden *minbar* that has survived from the earliest days of Islam.

To the left of the *minbar*, is the equally beautiful carved marble *mihrab* (prayer

ناجي

On the upper part of the *mihrab* and walls on either side are more than one hundred superb ceramic lustre tiles. These were also made by master craftsmen in Baghdad. (See illustration on page 11)

'Uqba ibn Nafi was a pious Muslim who spent the rest of his life spreading the message of Islam to the people of *Ifriqiya*. 'Uqba travelled as far as the coast of the Atlantic Ocean (in present-day Morocco). There, he rode his horse into the pounding ocean waves and asked Allah to be his witness:

> *O, Allah! If this sea of darkness had not appeared before me, I would have conveyed Your Name , which is the source of light, to the most remote corners of the world.*

Masha'Allah, 'Uqba ibn Nafi kept his word and did indeed carry the message of Islam to the extreme limits of his world. Today, the country of Morocco is called in Arabic *al-maghreb al-'aqsa'* , "the land of the farthest west"!

QUESTIONS

1. How far had Islam spread one generation after the death of the Prophet Muhammad Œ?

2. What did the Umayyad Caliph Mu'awiyya do in 670 CE?

3. Where was the province of *Ifriqiya*?

4. Who accompanied 'Uqba ibn Nafi and his army when he arrived in North Africa?

5. What kind of city did 'Uqba ibn Nafi hope Qayrawan would become?

6. What are the four holy cities of Islam?

7. For what purposes was the Sidi 'Uqba Mosque used in the early days of Islam?

8. What is so special about the minaret of the Sidi 'Uqba Mosque?

9. What did 'Uqba ibn Nafi do when he reached the shores of the Atlantic Ocean?

10. What country today is called "the land of the farthest west"?

Topic for Discussion: Discuss in detail the importance of the city of Qayrawan in the history of Islamic art and architecture.

3. Birth of Islamic Coinage – 695 CE

As mentioned earlier, during the lifetime of the Prophet ﷺ, the two superpowers of the day were the Byzantine (East Roman) and Sasanian (Persian) empires. Arabia was still a traditional trade and barter society and, therefore, had little need for coinage. In neighbouring lands, however, there were two very important coins in usage: the Byzantine gold *solidus* and the Sasanian silver *drachm*. The Prophet ﷺ surely must have seen such coins when he conducted his trading missions to *balad al-sham* (Syria) on behalf of Hadhrat Khadeejah (*radhi Allah-u 'anha*).

What were the first truly Islamic coins like? Where were they first minted (struck/ stamped)? Why are these coins important?

After the death of the Prophet ﷺ in 632 CE, Islam very quickly spread in all directions: east towards Sasanian Persia and north and west to the Byzantine lands. The Muslim governors of these new Islamic territories continued to mint the same old gold and copper Byzantine coins (showing the emperor and the Christian cross) and the famous large silver Sasanian *drachm* (showing the Sasanian monarch and the Zoroastrian fire temple altar).

By the time of the Caliph 'Uthman (*radhi Allah-u 'anhu*) [644-656 CE], Arabic inscriptions such as *bismillah* were being stamped around the wide margin of the Sasanian silver coins. The rest of the coin remained the same; it showed the crowned head of the Persian king and interesting pre-Islamic *Pahlavi* inscriptions.

These coins could be called Islamic because of the addition of such Arabic phrases on them. It was, however, during the reign of the fifth Umayyad caliph, 'Abd al-Mailk ibn Marwan (646-705 CE), that "original" Islamic coins were struck for the first time.

'Abd al-Malik ibn Marwan in his capital Damascus, introduced many important reforms. For example, he proclaimed Arabic the official language of the new Islamic Empire, replacing the Byzantine Greek, *Pahlavi* (Persian), Syraic and Coptic (Egyptian) languages. He also standardized the weights of the new gold *dinar* and silver *dirham*.

'Abd al-Malik ibn Marwan struck the first Islamic *dirham* in 695 CE (75 AH). *Masha'Allah*, what a beautiful coin it was! For the first time, Islamic coinage had an Arabic inscription devoid of any human or animal image.

These early Islamic coins are very religious in character. The obverse (the side of the coin with the most important

The early Islamic coins.

stamp) bears the first part of the *kalimah al-shahadah* in beautiful Kufic script.

On the reverse of these coins is inscribed the "mission statement" (*surah al-tawbah - ayah 33*):

> *Muhammad is the messenger of Allah who sent him with guidance and the religion of truth that He might make it supreme over all other religions.*

The *ayahs* of *surah al-ikhlas* are also inscribed: *qul hu Allah-u ahad*. The great beauty and importance of such coins can still be appreciated by Muslims today. The silver *dirham* illustrated here is from the time of 'Abd al-Malik ibn Marwan. The inscription of the top coin is very easy to read.

If we begin in the upper right-hand corner of the coin and continue to move anti-clockwise, the inscription reads: *bismillah dhuriba hadha al-dirham bi dimashq fi sannah wahad wa thamanin. Dhuriba* , of course, means "hit", "struck" or "minted". So, the coin reads, "In the name of Allah, this *dirham* was struck (minted) in Damascus in the year 81 (AH)."

The new coins minted during the time of 'Abd al-Malik were dedicated to Allah. Each coin was in fact a *da'i*, an Islamic missionary, inviting all who held it to *din al-haq al-islam*.

It is important to note that these early Islamic coins influenced the design and weight of all Islamic coinage for a thousand years.

With 'Abd al-Malik, the custom of placing the name of God on coinage began – a practice that survives to this day,even in America!

QUESTIONS

1. Why was there no need for local coinage in Arabia during the time of the Prophet ﷺ?

2. What were the two important coins in usage during the time of the Prophet ﷺ?

3. What coins were used by Muslims after the death of the Prophet ﷺ when Islam spread east and west?

4. What images did the Sasanian silver *drahma* coins show?

5. When was the *bismillah* first placed on an Islamic coin?

6. When and by whom were the first truly Islamic coins minted?

7. Identify two important reforms introduced by Caliph 'Abd al-Malik ibn Marwan.

8. What complete *surah* was inscribed on the new silver *dirhams* of 'Abd al-Malik ibn Marwan.

9. What does the Arabic verb *dhuriba* mean?

10. What is the most important legacy of these early Islamic coins?

Topic for Discussion: Compare and contrast the Islamic coinage of 'Abd al-Malik ibn Marwan (see illustration) with the coins you have in your own pocket.

4. Tariq ibn Ziyad – 711 CE

We have all heard of the great cultural accomplishments of Muslim Spain. How and when, however, did *al-din al-haq al-islam* arrive in this part of southern Europe and what was the real legacy of Muslim rule?

In the late 7th century CE, southern Spain (al-Andalus) was the most westerly outpost of the Roman Catholic world. (The Arabic word *al-andalus* probably derives from *Vandalicia*, a name given to southern Spain by the Vandals, a Germanic people that invaded Spain between the 4th and 5th centuries CE.) Another Germanic people, the Visogoths, ruled Spain and made the lives of their subjects – Christians and Jews – miserable. People had to pay many taxes and large farms were worked by serfs whose conditions were worse than those of slaves.

By the early 8th century CE, all of North Africa was under Muslim control. Musa ibn Nasayr was the Arab governor of this region. He represented the Umayyad Caliph Walid ibn 'Abd al-Malik ibn Marwan who resided in Damascus. Musa lived in Ceuta (*Sabta*), a small seaport on the Moroccan coast from which Spain could be seen on a clear day. He decided to extend *dar al-islam* by sending Muslims across the straits into Al-Andalus.

The people inhabiting North Africa at this time were the Berbers. The governor of Tangiers (another port city of northern Morocco) was a new Muslim, the Berber Tariq ibn Ziyad. Musa chose Tariq to lead an army of 7,000 Berbers into Al-Andalus. The specific date of this historic moment was April 28, 711 CE (5 *Rajab* 692 AH).

Tariq ibn Ziyad boarded one of his ships (see illustration) in the evening and landed on Spanish soil the next morning where he offered his *fajr* prayer. Tariq first captured the mountain previously called *jabal al-fath* ("mountain of conquest") which was renamed *jabal tariq* ("Tariq's mountain" or Gibraltar). Two months later at the end of Ramadhan 92 AH (July 711 CE), the Muslims now numbering 12,000 faced the Visigothic army of king Roderick on a river plain to the west of Gibraltar.

Tariq told his soldiers to be brave in battle:

> *O, Muslims! To where can you flee? With the sea behind you and your enemy in front, by Allah, it is your courage and patience alone that can help you.*

Historians, both Arab and Christian, agree that Visigoths opposed to the new king Roderick, helped the Muslims in their invasion of Al-Andalus.

طارق
ناجي

After a week-long battle, Roderick was left dead and his army defeated. Musa ibn Nasayr then wrote a letter to the Caliph Walid I in Damascus and described Tariq's first battle with king Roderick:

Ya, amir al-mu'minin ! These are not common conquests; they are like the meeting of nations on the Day of Judgement.

Tariq continued his conquests; both Toledo, the Visigothic capital, and Cordoba fell to the Muslims and within a decade, almost the whole of Spain was under their control.

What was the legacy of Tariq ibn Ziyad's stunning victory? First, the Muslim conquest of Spain brought about truly revolutionary changes to the lives of the Christians and Jews living there. The Muslims showed respect for property and tolerated the freedom of religious practice. Christians and Jews were able to worship in their churches and synagogues without fear of any persecution. Non-Muslims paid a *jaziyah* tax and were thus fully protected by the Muslim state and did not need to serve in the Muslim army. Muslim administrators also very quickly set a precedent: they kept their promise and applied justice equally to all.

The Visigothic serfs who had once worked on the land like slaves, were now freed. They could farm the land after giving a portion of their crops to the Muslim state. Because of this freedom, Muslim Spain soon became an agricultural paradise: a land of luxuriant gardens which produced every imaginable kind of fruit and vegetable.

Within a century of Tariq's landing on Spanish soil, Arabic quickly became the language of culture; even Christians and Jews preferred it. Over time, the Arabs, Berbers and local Spanish Muslims became one unified Muslim population. During the reign of the Caliph 'Abd al-Rahman III in the 10th century CE, Al-Andalus became the most important centre for learning in all of Europe.

Perhaps the most important consequence of the 800-year-long Muslim presence in Al-Andalus were the periods of peaceful co-existence between Muslims, Christians and Jews. Great tolerance was shown by many Muslim governments to their Christian and Jewish minorities. This tolerance led to a long period of cultural creativity. For centuries, Christian scholars came to Al-Andalus to study at Muslim centres of learning. Many famous Jewish scholars of Muslim Spain such as Musa ibn Maymun (Moses Maimonides) wrote important works in Arabic that are still valued today.

Finally, it must be said that at the end of Muslim rule in Spain in the late 15th century CE, Spanish Christians *sadly* never showed Muslims the same tolerance and respect for their religious rights that Muslims had once shown to the Christians and Jews of Spain.

QUESTIONS

1. What is the origin of the word *Al-Andalus*?

2. What two religious groups lived in pre-Islamic Spain?

3. Why were the people in pre-Islamic Spain unhappy with Visigothic rule?

4. Who was Musa ibn Nasayr?

5. Who was Tariq ibn Ziyad?

6. What does *jabal tariq* mean in English?

7. What was one important result of Tariq's conquest of Spain that benefited the local people?

8. Why did Arabic become the language of culture in Al-Andalus?

9. When did Al-Andalus become the most important centre of learning in all of Europe?

10. What was the direct result of the peaceful co-existence of Christians, Jews and Muslims in Spain?

Topic for Discussion: Identify and describe the many changes in Spainish society that occurred as a result of the arrival of Tariq ibn Ziyad.

5. The Battle of Talas – Papermaking – 751 CE

In ancient Egyptian times, the papyrus plant was used to make a simple form of paper. In lands distant from Egypt, stretched animal skins called parchment were used to write on.

The first real paper, as we know it today, was invented in China almost 2,000 years ago. For many centuries, the Chinese were the only suppliers of this commodity. Chinese paper was easy to make but its manufacture was kept a secret. First, pieces of bamboo and the under-bark of the mulberry tree were chopped and beaten into a pulp. This was then soaked in a mixture of water and wood ash. The pulp was spread in an even layer on a flat screen or sieve and left to drain. Finally, the sheet of paper was picked up, smoothed and left to dry.

By the middle of the 8th century CE, Muslims had settled in lands from far-off Spain in the west to Central Asia in the east. In 751 CE, the mighty army of the Chinese T'ang Dynasty confronted the combined forces of Arabs and Turks (led by Ziyad ibn Salih, an 'Abbasid commander) in a remote area of Central Asia. The battle took place near the Talas River (present-day Kirghizstan). This was the first time a world empire of the East (China) clashed directly with a world empire of the West (Islamic).

The Battle of Talas was a victory for Islam and proved to be of great historical importance. First, it helped expand Islam into Central Asia and brought new people and their culture into the *ummah*. After the Battle of Talas, Islamic rule became firmly established in the region and by the 10th century CE, Central Asia had became a vibrant new centre of Islamic culture. Cities like Kashgar, Balkh, Samarqand, Tashkent and Merv were home to many gifted scholars and artisans.

During the Battle of Talas, two Chinese papermakers were captured. They bargained for their freedom by agreeing to reveal the closely-guarded secret of papermaking to their Arab captors. The papermakers were taken south to Samarqand where quality paper was soon produced in vast quantities. By 793 CE, paper was being made in the mills in Baghdad, the new 'Abbasid capital.

Information could now be recorded and distributed at very little expense; for the first time in history, books were within reach of everyone. Documents of all kinds were written on paper, replacing the more costly papyrus and parchment. Paper had many obvious advantages. It absorbed ink and was therefore difficult to erase. Baghdad soon became a city with a lively papermakers' market (*suq al-warraqin*)

ناجی

where dozens of shops sold books and stationery supplies. Books of every kind could now be produced inexpensively. The important collections of *ahadeeth*, traditions of the Prophet ﷺ, were now written in ink on paper for the first time. Separate sheets were bound together to form books as we know them today.

The Qur'an, however, was still written on more expensive sheets of parchment, but by the early 14th century CE, master papermakers in Baghdad had perfected newer techniques for producing a finer quality paper. Beautifully made large (72 cm x 50 cm) sheets of polished paper were now used by master calligraphers to copy the Holy Qur'an in a wide range of exquisite handwriting styles. *Al-Hamdulillah*, many superb examples of early Islamic paper can be seen today in museums. The great skill of both papermakers and calligraphers can be admired and appreciated.

Over the centuries, the hand-made manufacture of paper was further developed by the Arabs and Turks. The Fatimids of Egypt were making paper by the year 1000 CE and by the end of the next century it was being made in Morocco and Al-Andalus. It wasn't until the 13th century CE, however, that the Europeans finally discovered the secret of papermaking.

Muslims were clearly important in transferring the knowledge of papermaking to Europe. Remember the Battle of Talas the next time you put pen to paper!

QUESTIONS

1. What is the difference between papyrus and parchment?

2. Where and when was the first real paper invented?

3. What were the ingredients of Chinese paper?

4. What event took place in 751 CE?

5. What was so unique about the Battle of Talas?

6. What important Chinese prisoners were taken after the Battle of Talas?

7. How did the discovery of papermaking by the Arabs affect the average person at the time?

8. What is one obvious advantage of paper over papyrus and parchment?

9. What are *ahadeeth* and when were they first written on paper?

10. Why was the Holy Qur'an not written on paper until the beginning of the 14th century CE?

Topic for Discussion: Discuss how you think the art of papermaking might have reached non-Muslim Europe?

6. Bayt al-Hikmah – Baghdad – 813-833 CE

With the advent of Islam in the 7th century CE, Muslims were encouraged by the Prophet ﷺ to "seek knowledge, even if it be in China" and by the Holy Qur'an "to read" (*iqra'*). It is truly an amazing fact that very soon after the secret of papermaking was made known to Muslims in 751 CE, *Dar al-Islam* became a land of avid readers and writers.

In 762 CE, Baghdad was founded as the capital of the new 'Abbasid dynasty. Its location was on the west side of the Tigris River, not far from the pre-Islamic Sasanian capital of Ctesiphon (Arabic *Mada'in*).

To the west of Baghdad, lay the former ancient Greek world and to the east were the Persian-speaking lands. Great libraries from these areas still existed in the early Islamic period. The libraries of Constaninople (the Byzantine Greek capital – present-day Istanbul in Turkey) and Edessa (present-day Shanli-Urfa in south east Turkey) housed valuable manuscripts written in Greek and Syriac (an ancient Aramaic language spoken in Syria). Moreover, Jundi-Shapur, the great Sasanian school of learning lying to the south east of Baghdad had a library overflowing with *Pahlavi* (Old Persian) manuscripts.

The 'Abbasid caliphs residing in Baghdad were the first Muslim rulers to become interested in the translation of such books into Arabic. For example, the second 'Abbasid caliph, al-Mansur (754-755 CE) studied astrology (the belief that planets and stars can influence human affairs) as a pastime. He had an ancient Indian mathematical book, the *Brahmasphuta Siddhanta* translated from Sanskrit (the ancient sacred language of India) into Arabic. Thus began a serious effort to purchase and collect manuscripts on astrology, medicine and other fields of sciences from various sources, Eastern or Western.

The Caliph al-Mansur's agents returned from foreign lands with many books that were quickly translated and placed in the caliph's reference library. One such book, *The Construction and Usage of the Astrolabe*, influenced European astronomy for centuries.

The famous caliph Harun al-Rashid (768-809 CE) continued the 'Abbasid tradition of collecting scientific manuscripts for translation. His library, the "Treasure of Knowledge" (*kanz al-hikmah*) soon housed thousands of books. Translators, both Muslim and non-Muslims, were kept very busy and contented. Exceptionally well-translated works were weighed and their weight in gold was given as wages to the translators!

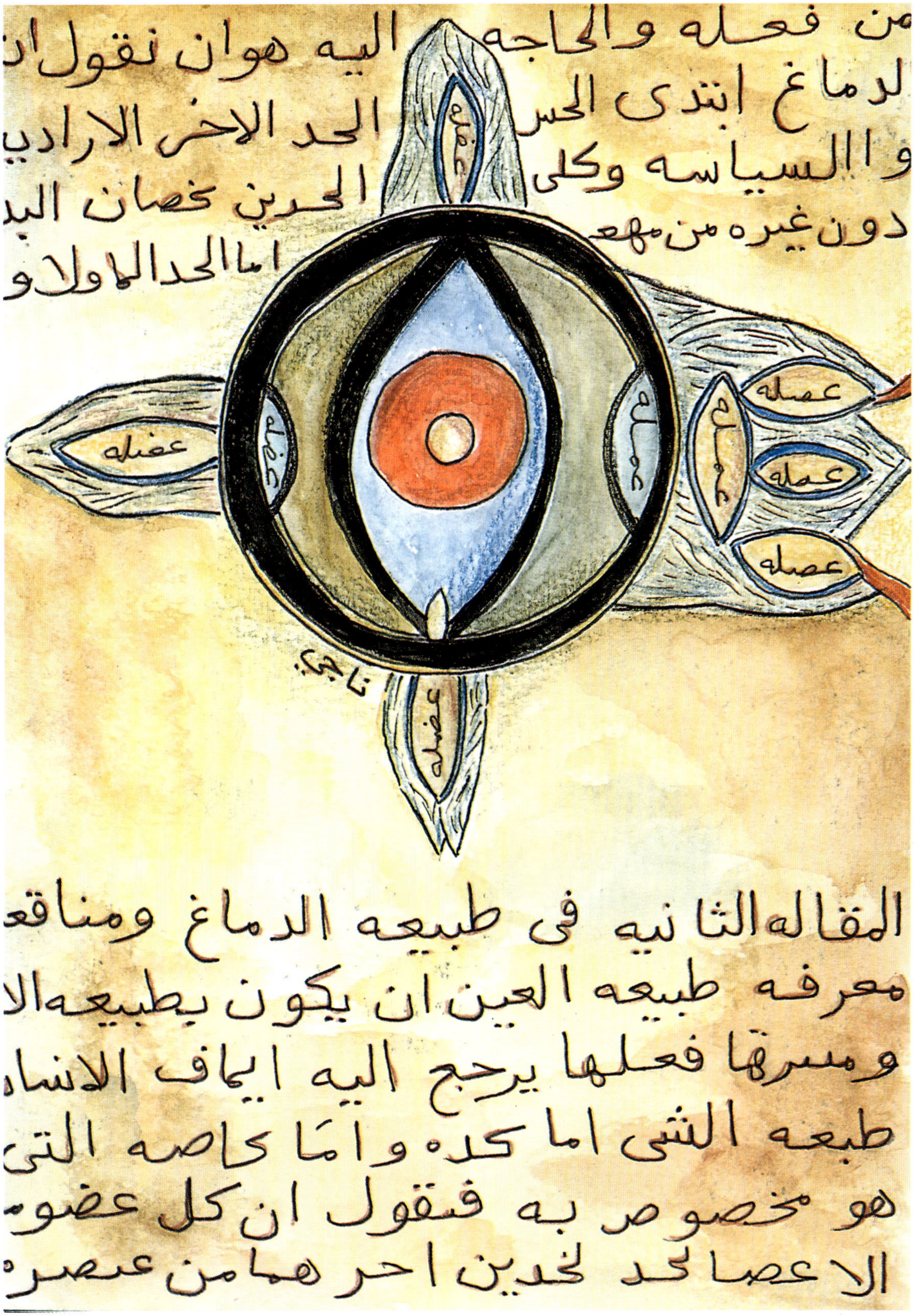
من فعله والحاجه اليه هوان نقول ان
الدماغ ابتدى الحس الحد الاخر الارادي
والسياسه وكلى الحدين خصان البد
دون غيره من مهع
اما الحد الاول و
عضله
عضله
عضله
عضله
عضله
عضله
عضله
عضله
عضله
ناجي
المقاله الثانيه فى طبيعه الدماغ ومناقع
معرفه طبيعه العين ان يكون يطبيعه الا
ومسرتها فعلها يرجع اليه ايهاف الانسا
طبعه الشى اما كده واما كاصه التى
هو مخصوص به فنقول ان كل عضو
الاعصا كد لخدين احرهما من عنصر

However, it was the Caliph al-Ma'mun (813-833 CE), the son of Harun al-Rashid, who became the greatest supporter of philosophy and science in all of Islamic history. A larger and more official institution, the "House of Knowledge" (*bayt al-hikmah*), was established by al-Ma'mun.

Only the very best translators and scholars worked in the *Bayt al-Hikmah*, comprising a library and an academy. In short, the aim of this institution was a mammoth one: to faithfully translate the body of philosophical and scientific knowledge that had survived from the Classical World (Greece and Rome). This wealth of information then had to be incorporated by scholar/translators into the new religion of Islam. The *Bayt al-Hikmah* (which survived in tact for only about fifty years) and the work of its hundreds of researchers left behind a very important legacy.

Scholars like Hunayn ibn Ishaq (809-873 CE), a director of the *Bayt al-Hikmah*, meticulously translated all extant Greek medical books into Arabic. These included the famous "Hippocratic Oath" that medical doctors the world over still accept today. Hunayn ibn Ishaq later began writing his own original medical works in Arabic. One such book discussed ophthalmology (the study of the eye), the anatomy (structure) of the eye and the treatment for various eye diseases.

A page showing an illustration from ibn Ishaq's book on the anatomy of the eye is presented here. This was the first time a medical book contained such drawings. For many centuries, this book in a Latin translation was used as a textbook by medical students at universities in both Europe and *Dar al-Islam*.

It is true to say that world culture has been made richer because of the work of these exceptional scholars. If the early 'Abbasid caliphs had not shown an interest in preserving the scientific knowledge of the ancient world, it could have been lost forever. It is unfortunate, however, that this Muslim link in the preservation and transfer of ancient knowledge is often overlooked by the West.

QUESTIONS

1. What do the Qur'an and *ahadeeth* tell Muslims about seeking knowledge?

2. Where were Baghdad and Ctesiphon located?

3. From what libraries could Muslims gather Greek and Syriac manuscripts?

4. What language was spoken and written by Sasanians?

5. Why was the Caliph al-Mansur important in the history of translating?

6. Who was Harun al-Rashid and what was the name of his library?

7. What is the name of the ancient sacred language of India?

8. What was the reward for excellent translation work?

9. Who was al-Ma'mun and what was the name of his library?

10. Why do we remember Hunayn ibn Ishaq?

Topic of Discussion: Compare and contrast the causes and effects of the first information explosion in Baghdad in the 9th century CE with the second information explosion in the late 20th century CE.

7. Al-Idrisi's Map of the World – 1154 CE

Muslims continued to discover important scientific works of antiquity from the Greek, Roman and Persian worlds to translate into Arabic. Although many of the books discussed mathematics, medicine and philosophy, Muslim scholar/translators also became interested in classical works of geography.

Ptolemy's *Geographia*, for example, was probably translated into Arabic from the original Greek at the court of Harun al-Rashid in Baghdad. As a direct result of the translation of this book, many Arab scholars began to write similar works bearing the title "Book of the Description of the Earth" (*kitab surat al-ardh*). One such geographical work was written in the *Bayt al-Hikmah* by al-Khwarizmi, the famous mathematician.

By the 9th century CE, Muslims had become familiar with many varied regions of the world: from Spain in the west to India and the seaports of China in the east. Arab cartographers ("mapmakers") now began to incorporate this newly-found knowledge when drawing their own maps.

Medieval Europe never accepted the Muslim presence in Al-Andalus (Spain and Portugal) and Sicily; they waited for the opportunity to retake these lands and restore them to the Christian world.

Between 1066 and 1071 CE, Norman (French) kings began to rule in southern Italy and on the island of Sicily. The Norman king of Sicily, Roger II (1097-1154 CE) ruled from his capital Palermo. This exceptional ruler appreciated the Islamic contribution to knowledge and welcomed Arab scholars to his palace.

In 1099 CE, in the Moroccan port city of Ceuta (*Sabta*), the home of Musa ibn Nasayr, was born the greatest geographer and cartographer of the Middle Ages: Abu 'Abd Allah Al-Sharif Al-Idrisi al-Qurtubi. After receiving his education in Cordoba (Spain), Al-Idrisi began to travel the world. Although not as travelled as Ibn Batutta (also a Moroccan), Al-Idrisi did visit many parts of the Middle East, Constantinople, Central Asia and even France and England.

King Roger, hearing of Al-Idrisi and his many skills, invited him to Palermo to help compile a book containing all the known information about the precise locations of places on the map of the world.

Al-Idrisi and other scholars in Palermo took fifteen years to complete the book known as *Al-Kitab al-Rujari* ("Roger's Book"). Al-Idrisi dedicated his work to his patron, King Roger. In 1154, King Roger himself gave the book a name: *Nuzhat al-Mushtaq fee Ikhtiraq al-Afaq* ("The Delights

جنوب
ناجي
شمال

of Him who desires to Journey through the Climes"); Al-Idrisi, however, decided to call it *Al-Kitab al-Rujari*. Because of his extended stay at the court of King Roger, some Muslims referred to Al-Idrisi as a "renegade". At the same time, the Arabic-speaking, Islamized Roger was often known as "the Pagan" by Christian historians. Clearly, both individuals were far ahead of their time in their understanding of religious tolerance and co-existence.

Arab geographers before Al-Idrisi had correctly measured the surface of the Earth. For example, the geographer Ibn Hawqal in the late 11th century CE, had produced a map of the whole world. Using these Arabic manuscripts, much older Greek charts and sailing manuals, as well as information obtained by personal experience, Al-Idrisi began to compile his book.

What made Al-Idrisi's book and maps so remarkable? Compared with similar works produced in the 12th century CE, Al-Idrisi's maps contained much greater detail. His knowledge of the sub-Saharan salt trade in the *Sahel* countries, for example, was very accurate. Al-Idrisi also placed the source of the Nile River in east Africa in the *jibaal al-qamar* ("mountains of the moon") which can be clearly seen on the copy of his map here. It is amazing that the precise origin of the Western Nile was not discovered by Europeans until the 19th century CE! Al-Idrisi was totally convinced that the Earth was spherical. For the skeptics who believed the water of the oceans could never remain on a curved surface, he answered that "an equilibrium which experiences no variation" keeps these bodies of water in place.

It is the cross-fertilization of cultures (the Arabs learning from the Greeks and subsequently bequeathing this knowledge to the West) that is the true legacy of geographers like Al-Idrisi. Even centuries later, Al-Idrisi's maps were available in libraries of European schools of navigation. Portuguese and Spanish explorers thus made use of them before setting out across the Atlantic Ocean (the "Sea of Darkness"). An important question can now be asked: Could Christopher Columbus have succeeded in his westerly voyages without the aid of Al-Idrisi's map?

QUESTIONS

1. From what branches of knowledge did early Muslim scholars translate books into Arabic?

2. What was the importance of the translation of Ptolemy's *Geographia* from Greek into Arabic?

3. What do cartographers do?

4. What did Arab cartographers begin to do by the 9th century CE?

5. Who was the Norman king of Sicily and what was his capital?

6. Who is considered to be the greatest cartographer and geographer of the Middle Ages?

7. Why was Al-Idrisi invited to the court of King Roger?

8. Why was Al-Idrisi's map of the world so special?

9. Did Al-Idrisi's map correctly show the source of the Nile River?

10. In the 12th century CE, many people thought the Earth was flat. What did Al-Idrisi believe?

Topic for Discussion: How important do you think Al-Idrisi's work has been to the history of world knowledge?

8. Destruction of Baghdad – 1258 CE

Since its founding in the 8th century CE, Baghdad had been a city of culture boasting famous palaces, mosques, *madrasahs*, hospitals and hundreds of libraries, public and private, big and small. It was the capital of the 'Abbasid dynasty for almost five hundred years. Great caliphs, *vizirs*, writers, philosophers, religious leaders all resided there. Imam Al-Ghazali taught at the reknowned *Nizamiyyah* College and Abu Hanifah (*radhi Allah-u 'anhu*), *al-imam al-adham*, lived and died in Baghdad.

The 'Abbasid themselves called their circular city with three inner walls, *Dar al-Salaam* (the "House of Peace"). In the centre was the Caliph's palace and the Grand Mosque. Baghdad was truly a city of knowledge where books of all kinds were translated, copied and bound, using the very best means available. Only Cordoba in far-off Al-Andalus could vie with the greatness of caliphal Baghdad.

By the middle of the 13th century CE, *Dar al-Islam* lacked unity. Even the 'Abbasid state had become weak. The Islamic world was divided into scores of small independent dynasties like the Ghorids, Ghaznavids and Samanids in the East and the Seljuqs of Rum, Ayyubids and Muwahhids in the West.

Many areas of Central Asia had suffered in the early 13th century CE at the hands of Genghis Khan (the "scourge of God"), the savage Mongol leader. By the middle of the century, his grandson Hulagu Khan was ready to continue the Mongol raids of death and destruction. The Mongols were a wild nomadic people whose homeland was in present-day Mongolia. They were superb horsemen and with Genghis Khan began to plunder lands in the west. They practiced Shamanism, an old animistic religion, but Hulagu Khan's wife and mother were both Nestorian Christians.

Hulagu's army was comprised of soldiers from all over the Mongol Empire. All the great Islamic cities of Central Asia and Persia soon fell to this conqueror. 'Ala al-Din al-Juwayni (died 1283 CE), the great Persian historian of the Mongol invasions, actually travelled with Hulagu Khan during his invasion of Persia. In his famous history of the Mongol conquests, Al-Juwayni wrote one very memorable sentence describing precisely how these barbarians attacked cities: "They came, they burned, they slaughtered, they looted, and then left."

The last 'Abbasid caliph, al-Must'asim bi Allah was arrogant and overconfident. He sent a message to Hulagu Khan in which he tried to frighten him into believing that an

كتاب الجبر
والمقابلة
محمد ابن مسى
الخوارزمي
ΞΕΝΟΦΩΝΤΟΣ

attack on Baghdad would mobilize the entire Muslim world. Hulagu continued to amass forces and when al-Must'asim realized how serious the threat was, it was too late for him to do anything.

Al-Must'asim tried to negotiate with Hulagu offering him the title of sultan and proposing that his name be mentioned in the Friday *khutbahs* in Baghdad. Hulagu Khan, however, was determined to attack and on February 10, 1258, Baghdad, the city of scholars and saints, fell to the Mongol horde.

It is no exaggeration to say that hundreds of thousands of innocent people lost their lives. The entire city was set alight and massacring and wanton destruction continued for days. The caliph was forced to surrender his treasure, but was still killed along with members of his family. According to the religious laws of the Mongols, royal blood could not be spilled. Historians therefore agree that the last of the 'Abbasid caliphs was likely rolled up in a carpet and trampled to death by horses.

The illiterate Mongol hordes ransacked palaces, homes and libraries. It is said that the water of the Tigris River first ran red with the blood of the dead and then black with the ink of the thousands of priceless manuscripts that were thrown into it. (See illustration.) The carefully translated hand-written books from the *Bayt al-Hikmah* and hundreds of other libraries – the collected knowledge of hundreds of years – were all destroyed in a matter of days. Sadly, Muslim disunity in *Dar al-Islam* preventd any help coming to the aid of *amir al-mu'minun*, the Caliph Must'asim.

Over the years, many historians have questioned why this disaster befell the *ummah*. Many believe that the society had become decadent and like the pruning of trees, the Mongols came and with their destruction made way for a new beginning.

The same catastrophe, however, did not befall the Mamluks of Egypt. In 1260 CE, Hulagu and the Mamluk forces met in Galilee ('ain jalut) in Palestine. This *jihad* was led by the Mamluk sultan Baybars himself. Hulagu Khan never reached Egypt but was defeated and in two years was forced to leave Palestine/Syria. Truly, Allah helps those who turn to Him. *Masha'Allah*, history writes that within a generation, the sons of Hulagu and all subsequent *Ilkhan* rulers had become Muslim, *al-Hamdulillah*. Uljaytu Khan (died 1316 CE), for example, also became a patron of Islamic arts. While his grandfather had shown no respect for learning, Uljaytu as a Muslim encouraged the copying of the Holy Qur'an in his palace.

QUESTIONS

1. Name two important Muslims who lived in Baghdad during its golden age?

2. What did the 'Abbasids call their beautiful capital city?

3. What was the condition of *Dar al-Islam* in the middle of the 13th century CE?

4. Who was Genghis Khan and who was his grandson?

5. Where did the Mongols come from and what was their ancestral religion?

6. Who was Al-Juwayni and what memorable words has he left us about the Mongol invasions?

7. Who was the last 'Abbasid caliph and how did he try to prevent Hulagu Khan from attacking Baghdad?

8. When did Hulagu and his army attack Baghdad and what was the result of the invasion?

9. What was the fate of Caliph Must'asim, Baghdad's inhabitants and the contents of the city's many great libraries?

10. From the brief information presented here, what was the main difference between the 'Abbasid caliph Must'asim and the Mamluk sultan Baybars?

Topic for Discussion: Do you really believe, as some historians do, that there was any positive outcome of Hulagu's barbarous destruction of Baghdad?

9. Conquest of Istanbul – 1453 CE

Istanbul, the former capital of the Ottoman Turkish Empire, is unique in many ways. It is the only city that lies on two continents: Europe and Asia. Founded more than 2,000 years ago, it became the seat of the Eastern Roman Empire or Byzantium, in 330 CE. The city became famous for its beauty, wealth and cultured inhabitants.

From the earliest days of Islam, the Byzantine Greek capital *Constantinopolis* (the "city of Constantine" or *Kustantiniyyah* in Ottoman Turkish and Arabic) had been a city that had eluded capture by Muslims. In 1071 CE, the Byzantine Emperor Romanos Diogenes confronted the army of the Seljuq Turks at Malazgirt, present-day eastern Turkey. The Seljuq Turks were a nomadic group of Turkish-speaking tribes that had been slowly migrating west from their ancestral homeland in Mongolia. The Byzantines were defeated and over the next four centuries, Turks populated most of the Byzantine lands of Anatolia (Asia Minor) – the present-day country of Turkey. By the middle of the 15th century CE, Constantinople was still the Byzantine capital, but not for much longer.

The Turks, known as Ottomans, were now a unified people ruled by powerful sultans. A very young sultan, the twenty-year-old Muhammad II, son of Sultan Murad II, was determined to make Constantinople the centre of the world. In April 1453 CE, Sultan Muhammad II sent a message to the Byzantine emperor Constantine XI Palaeologus asking him to surrender to the Muslim forces. The emperor refused, so Muhammad II began his siege of the city which lasted fifty-three days.

Preparations for the attack had been made. A Hungarian weapons maker produced the most powerful cannons the world had ever seen. In the beginning, the Ottoman navy was prevented from entering the Golden Horn Strait because the Byzantines had cut it off with a huge chain. However, the Turks were not discouraged. Sultan Muhammad's spiritual teacher, Ak Shams al-Din, had predicted victory over Byzantime. Sultan Muhammad was a young, but very capable commander. Seventy Ottoman ships were moved overland, up and down the hills above the Golden Horn. They were pulled by oxen over well-greased wooden slipways and helped by hundreds of Turkish troops. Early in the morning, on May 28, 1453, the Ottomans began their final march towards Constantinople and by noon, the once powerful Greek capital of the Eastern

علي
محمد
الله
ابوبكر
ناجي

Christian world and the 1.125 years old Byzantine Empire had fallen to the forces of Islam.

Sultan Muhammad II was immediately given the title *al-fath*, "the conqueror". On May 30, 1453, he proceeded on horseback through the deserted streets of his new capital to the great Church of Holy Wisdom (*Haghia Sophia*). Upon entering this ancient church, Sultan Muhammad al-Fath proclaimed it the new *jami'i al-kabeer*, or Great Mosque. He led the first Friday payers there. Four large minarets were later added by four different sultans. Many of the interior walls covered with colourful tile mosaics were plastered over. Once the *qiblah* (direction of Makkah) had been determined, a marble *mihrab* (prayer niche) and *minbar* (pulpit) were built. Large circular wooden panels were painted with the words *Allah* and *Muhammad* in gold leaf. These were suspended from the dome above the *mihrab*. (See illustration.)

Sultan Muhammad al-Fath quickly began to make *Kustantiniyyah* a world capital. Palaces, mosques, *madrasahs*, public markets and baths were built. He encouraged the re-population of the city. Peoples from all over the Ottoman Empire were invited to reside in Istanbul. By the end of the 15th century CE, even Jews from as far away as Spain sought shelter from persecution there. Istanbul survived as a capital of the Turkish Empire until 1924 CE.

Muslims had always dreamed of occupying Constantinople. In the late 7th century CE, the Umayyad Caliph Mu'awiya had planned a campaign to capture the city. Yazid ibn Mu'awiya and even the eighty-year old beloved Companion of the Prophet ﷺ, Abu Ayyub al-Ansari (*radhi Allah-u 'anhu*) had accompanied the army north. On the plains some distance from Istanbul, Abu Ayyub al-Ansari (*radhi Allah-u 'anhu*) fell ill during a battle. Before his death, Yazid asked him his final wish: "Convey my *salaams* to all Muslims. Penetrate deep into enemy territory and bury me beneath the walls of *Kustantiniyyah*." Abu Ayyub al-Ansari (*radhi Allah-u 'anhu*) was indeed buried there as he had wished.

Eight hundred years later, Sultan Muhammad al-Fath prayed in the new mosque of *Haghia Sophia* (*Aya Sofya* in Turkish). He asked his religious teacher Ak Shams al-Din to show him the grave of Abu Ayyub al-Ansari (*radhi Allah-u 'anhu*). The burial place was soon discovered and Sultan Muhammad al-Fath had a mosque and a *madrasah* built near the site. Today, if one visits Istanbul, one can pray *salat al-dhuhr* in the *Haghia Sophia* Mosque and *salat al-'asr* in the Mosque of Abu Ayyub al-Ansari (*radhi Allah-u 'anhu*).

QUESTIONS

1. What is so special about the geographical location of Istanbul, the former Ottoman capital?

2. What are two other names for Istanbul?

3. What happened to this city in 330 CE?

4. What is the importance of the year 1071 CE in Turkish history?

5. Who was Muhammad II and what was his goal as a young sultan?

6. Who was the last Byzantine emperor and what was his reply to Muhammad II's message to him?

7. When the siege of Constantinople began, why was it difficult for the Turkish navy to enter the Golden Horn? How did they overcome the problem?

8. After the conquest of the city, what new name was given to Sultan Muhammad II?

9. What important changes did Sultan Muhammad al-Fath make to the ancient Byzantine Church of Holy Wisdom?

10. What did Sultan Muhammad al-Fath do to ensure that his city would become a "world capital"?

Topic for Discussion: How important do you think the life of Abu Ayyub al-Ansari (*radhi Allah-u 'anhu*) has been to the history of Istanbul?

10. The Fall of Granada – 1492 CE

The 800-year-long history of Muslim Spain is a fascinating one. As mentioned earlier, its "golden age" was unquestionably during the reign of the Umayyad Caliph 'Abd al-Rahman III (912-961 CE) who ruled from his newly-built palace city of *Madinah al-Zahra* outside of Cordoba. This was a time of extraordinary creative activity in all aspects of life. The cities of Al-Andalus were vibrant places of learning; Seville, Cordoba and Granada all had important libraries open day and night. The palace library of Hakam II reportedly housed over 400,000 books! Outside of Baghdad in the East, Islamic Spain had no rival.

Ibn Khaldun, the famous Tunisian, known as "the father of historiography/ sociology" wrote on the reasons for the rise and eventual decline of all cultures. That of Al-Andalus was no exception. When the Muslim *ummah* was united, it thrived; when disunited, it suffered defeat. The Spanish Umayyad Caliphate came to an end in about 1010 CE. After this time, Al-Andalus, the once mighty and prosperous "garden province" of the West, reverted to a land of dozens of rival "factional kings" (*al-muluk al-tawa'if*).

The Christian kings of northern Spain, of course, took full advantage of the situation in order to reclaim land from the Muslims. Over the centuries, Muslim city states (belonging to the *muluk al-tawa'if*) fell one by one into the hands of the Catholic monarchs. The *Beni Nasr* , or Nasrid rulers of Granada (*Gharnata*) survived the longest. They were able to protect their small province lying in the south-east of Spain despite being surrounded by Christian states.

Historians write of the last great flowering of Spanish Muslim culture taking place at this time. Nasrid rulers of the 13th century CE could not have predicted the fate of their descendents two centuries later. Granada, the capital of the Beni Nasr, soon became a microcosm of all that had once been so special about Al-Andalus. The arts flourished: beautiful Arabic poetry was still being composed; scientists wrote amazing books on all subjects; and architects built the most exquisite monuments in all of the western Islamic world. Some of these beautiful works of art exist to this very day.

The Nasrid princes lived in the famous "Alhambra" palace (from the Arabic *al-qasr al-hamra'* or "red palace") on a hilltop overlooking the well-irrigated gardens of Granada. Many experts agree that this palace (built during the 13th and 14th centuries CE), is the most outstanding

ناجي

example of Islamic art ever produced in this part of the Muslim world. History tells us that the Caliph 'Abd al-Rahman III had once returned victorious from battle. The inhabitants of Cordoba then welcomed him back home as "victor". 'Abd al-Rahman III quickly uttered the words : "There is no Victor but Allah!" (*wa la ghaliba ila Allah*). For several hundred years , *wa la ghaliba ila Allah* became the motto of the Beni Nasr. These words (see illustration) are repeated in beautiful Arabic calligraphy thousands of times on the carved stuccoed walls, ceilings and portals of the Alhambra palace. The Nasrid motto even appears on their coinage. (See illustration on page 3.)

The fate of the glorious Nasrid dynasty of Spain was sealed when the combined forces of Queen Isabella and King Ferdinand began to attack in the late 15th century CE. The last Nasrid ruler, Abu 'Abd Allah (called *Boabdil* by the Spanish), had wanted to live in peace with his Christian neighbours. It was decided that surrender to the Christian enemy would save the lives of many Muslims. Abu 'Abd Allah, thus accepted the conditions for peace presented to him by King Ferdinand. It must be said that Abu 'Abd Allah fought very hard to secure and safeguard the rights of his Muslim subjects. King Ferdinand had promised to respect these rights: Muslims in Spain under Christian control would be able to worship freely in mosques, would not be forced to become Christian, and could continue to speak Arabic and wear Islamic clothing without fear of persecution.

Therefore, Granada, the last flower of Muslim Spain, fell into the hands of the Spanish king on January 2, 1492. Within two years, however, King Ferdinand had gone back on his word. Muslims and Jews were forcibly converted to Christianity. They were forbidden from speaking Arabic or practicing any Muslim custom. This "ethnic cleansing" continued for one hundred years. Finally, in 1609 CE, Philip III of Spain expelled all remaining Muslims from Spanish territory. All traces of Muslim culture were shamefully erased: mosques became churches, graveyards were desecrated, and whole libraries of valuable literary treasures were burned in large public bonfires!

In 1992, the 500th anniversary of the Christian "reconquest" of Granada, the present Spanish king, Juan Carlos (a descendent of King Ferdinand), publicly apologized for the inhuman intolerance shown by his ancestors towards the Muslim community of Spain. Today, there are new mosques being built in many parts of southern Spain for the growing number of Muslims living there. *Al-Hamdulillah*, Islam has once again taken root in the soil of Al-Andalus, never again to be disinterred, *insha'Allah.*

QUESTIONS

1. When was the "golden age" of Muslim Spain and what were Spanish cities like then?

2. Who was Ibn Khaldun and what important lesson did he leave us in his writing?

3. When did the Umayyad Caliphate of Spain come to an end and what happened to Al-Andalus after this period?

4. What was the fate of many of the *muluk al-tawa'if* and their lands?

5. Who were the Beni Nasr and what were they able to do?

6. According to many historians, when and where did the last great flowering of Islamic culture in Spain take place?

7. What was the Nasrid capital and what is so special about the palace there?

8. What was the famous motto of the Beni Nasr and what was its history?

9. Who was Abu 'Abd Allah and what did he try to do before finally surrendering to King Ferdinand in 1492 CE?

10. What happened to Muslims two years after the fall of Granada?

Topic for Discussion: What important lessons can we learn from the tragic history of the Muslims of Al-Andalus?

Istanbul
Al-Andalus
Granada
Sicily
Gibraltar
Qâyrawan
North Africa
دار الاسلام
The World of Islam
ناجي

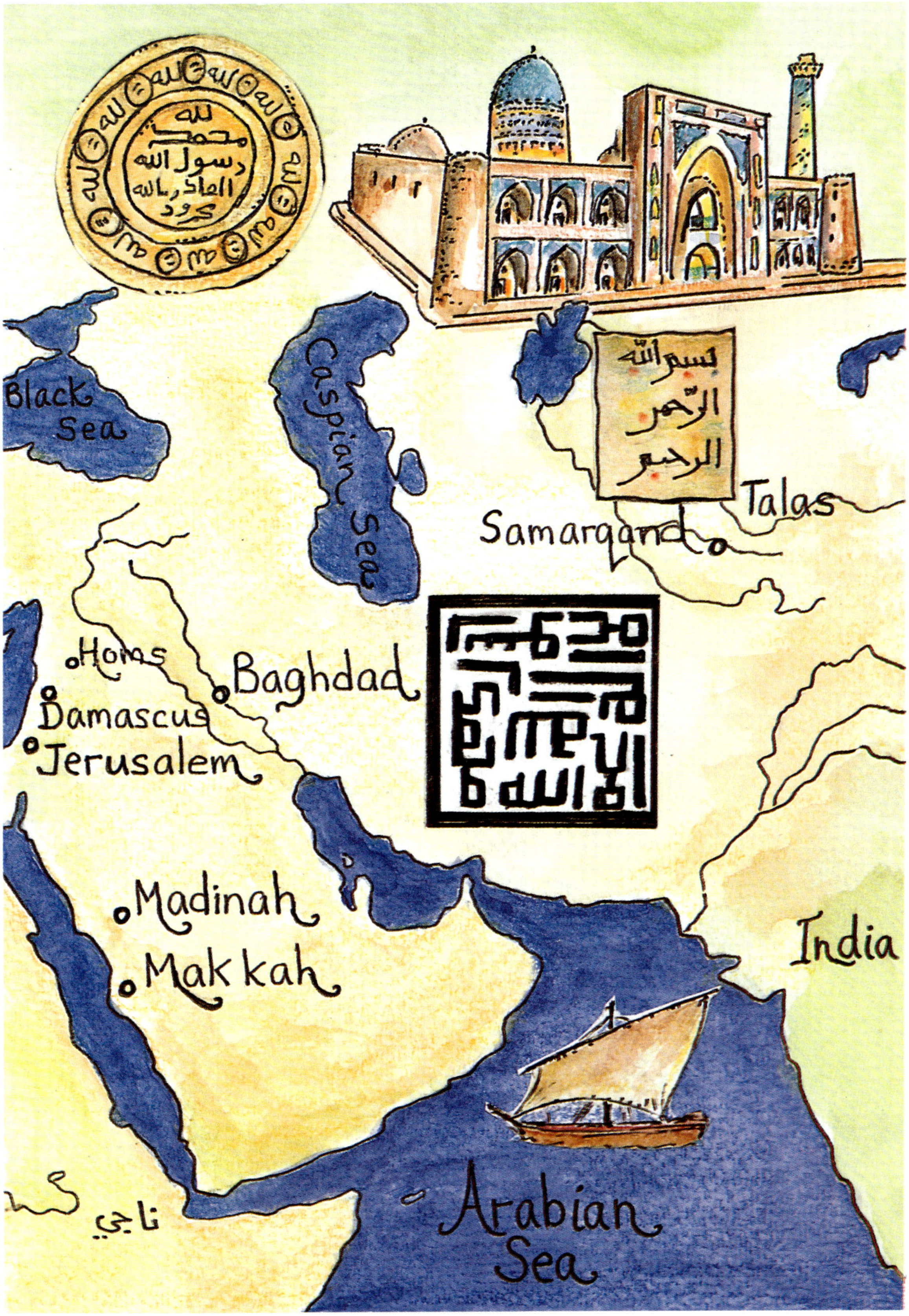
الله
محمد
رسول الله
بسم الله
الرحمن
الرحيم
Black Sea
Caspian Sea
Talas
Samarqand
Homs
Baghdad
Damascus
Jerusalem
Madinah
Makkah
India
Arabian Sea
ناجي

GLOSSARY

'Abbasid: the second Islamic dynasty that succeeded the Umayyads in 749 CE.

Ahadeeth: the collected "traditions" or reported deeds and sayings of the Prophet Muhammad ﷺ.

Amir al-Mu'minin: Arabic for "commander of the faithful"; the title given to many caliphs and kings of Islamic lands.

Al-Andalus: Arabic name for the area of Spain and Portugal that were once part of the Islamic world.

Ayah: Arabic for a verse of the Holy Qur'an.

Balad al-Sham: the area now comprising Syria, Palestine, Lebanon and Jordan.

Bayt al-Hikmah: the "translation bureau" established in Baghdad by the 'Abbasid caliph Al-Ma'mun in the 9th century CE.

Beni nasr: Arabic for "the sons of Nasr"; the Nasrids of Al-Andalus, the last great Muslim dynasty of Islamic Spain.

Bismillah: the Arabic ritual formula *bismillah al-rahman al-rahim* : "In the Name of Allah, the Merciful, the Compassionate".

Caliph: from the Arabic *khalifah* meaning viceroy or representative; the first four caliphs, 'Abu Bakr, 'Umar, 'Uthman, and 'Ali were known as *al-khulafa' al-rashidun* or "the rightly guided Caliphs".

Da'i: one who "calls or summons" to Islam; a Muslim missionary dar al-imara – Arabic for government administrative buildings.

Dhuriba: "was struck" passive form of Arabic verb "to strike" referring to the minting of Islamic coinage.

Dinar: an Islamic coin, mainly gold; from the Latin word denarius.

Dirham: an Islamic silver coin; from the Greek word drachma.

Drachm: large silver pre-Islamic Sasanian coin.

Al-fath: Arabic for "the Victorious"; an epithet given to many Islamic rulers throughout history.

Al-hamdulillah: Arabic for "praise be to Allah".

Ifriqiyah: Arabic name used in the early days of Islam to refer to the area now known as Tunisia in North Africa.

Ilkhan: a Mongol dynasty of Persia (Iran) founded by Hulagu Khan and later ruled by his sons and grandsons from 1256-1353 *insha'Allah* – Arabic for "if Allah wills".

Jabal: Arabic for "mountain".

Jami'i al-Kabeer: Arabic for "the large congregational [Friday] mosque".

Jaziyah: a tax paid by non-Muslim males living in Islamic lands; this tax exempted the payer from military service yet guaranteed his protection by the Islamic state.

Jibaal: Arabic for "mountains".

Jihad: Arabic for "holy struggle" in order to achieve spiritual perfection or a "holy struggle" against non-believers.

Kalimah al-Shahadah: Arabic for "the [Islamic] testimony of faith, i.e. "I bear witness that there is no Deity worthy of worship but Allah, and that Muhammad ﷺ is the Messenger of Allah".

Kanz al-hikmah: Arabic for "the treasure of knowledge", the library founded by Harun al-Rashid in Baghdad.

Al-Khulafa' al-Rashidun: Arabic for the "the rightly guided caliphs", namely the first four caliphs after the death of the Prophet Muhammad ﷺ.

Khutbah: Arabic for the "sermon" given in a mosque by an imam before Friday congregational prayers

Kitab surat al-Ardh: Arabic for "book showing the picture of the Earth", i.e. a descriptive atlas written by early Muslim mapmakers.

Mada'in: pre-Islamic capital city of Persian Sasanian Empire; near present-day Baghdad.

Madinah al-Zahra: ceremonial capital city of Spanish Umayyad caliph 'Abd al-Rahman III (10th century CE); outside of the city of Cordoba.

Madrasah: a traditional Islamic school.

Al-maghreb al-'Aqsa': Arabic for "the farthest west"; the classical name given to the country of Morocco.

Mihrab: Arabic for the "prayer niche" that indicates the *qiblah*, or the direction of Holy Makkah.

Minbar: Arabic for the mosque "pulpit" from which the imam reads the Friday sermon.

Masha' Allah: Arabic for "what Allah has willed".

Al-muluk al-Tawa'if: Arabic for the period of "factional kings"; the 400 years of Islamic history following the abolition of the Caliphate in Muslim Spain in 1031 CE.

Pahlavi: the pre-Islamic old Persian language of the Sasanian Empire.

Al-qasr al-Hamra': Arabic for "the red palace"; the palace of the Nasrid dynasty in Granada, Spain known in English as the "Alhambra".

Qiblah: Arabic word for the direction in which Muslims pray when offering *salah* (i.e. the *ka'bah* in Makkah).

Radhi Allah-u 'anhu ('anha, 'anhum): Arabic for "may Allah be pleased with him/her/them".

Sahel: Arabic for "coast"; name given to the semi-arid regions lying south of the Sahara Desert in north central Africa.

Sahih al-Bukhari: the important book of authentic *ahadeeth* compiled by Imam Al-Bukhari.

Salaam: Arabic for "peace"; the traditional Muslim greeting.

Salat al-'Asr: the afternoon congregational prayer.

Salat al-Dhuhr: the noon congregational prayer.

Salat al-Fajr: the morning congregational prayer.

Solidus: the typical gold coin of the Byzantine Empire.

Sunnah: Arabic for "custom" as applied to the habits, speech, and mannerisms of the Prophet ﷺ.

Suq al-Warraqin: Arabic for "market of paper sellers"; the famous market established in the 8th cent. CE Baghdad.

Surah: Arabic word for a chapter of the Holy Qur'an.

Ummah: Arabic word for "community or nation" traditionally referring to the "Islamic nation".

Umayyad: the first dynasty in Islamic history beginning with Mu'awiyah in 661 CE and ending with Marwan II in 750 CE.

Vizir: from Arabic "wazir" meaning an important government minister.

Wa la ghaliba ila Allah – Arabic for "and there is no Victor but Allah"; the famous motto of the Nasrid dynasty of Muslim Spain.

Zam zam: Arabic for the name of the well of sweet water located near the *ka'bah* in the Grand Mosque in Holy Makkah.

Ziyarah: Arabic for a "visit"; in Islam it is customary to make a visit to holy places like Makkah and Madinah.

Zoroastrian: adjective for Zoroaster, the founder of the religion called Zoroastrianism, the pre-Islamic fire-worshipping religion of the Persian Sasanian Empire.